# Impeccability

# of the

# Source Text

# in Translations

**Luis R. Cerna**

Bibliografische Informationen der Deutschen Nationalbibliothek:
Die Deutschen Nationalbibliothek verzeichnet diese Publikation in der
Deutschen Nationalbibliografie; detaillierte bibliografische
Daten sind im Internet über http://dnb.dnb.de abrufbar.


Publisher:
BoD · Books on Demand GmbH,
Überseering 33, 22297 Hamburg,
bod@bod.de
Print:
Libri Plureos GmbH,
Friedensallee 273, 22763 Hamburg

ISBN: 978-3-7693-5001-2

# Table of Contents

# 1. Antecedents

Years ago, during the training as student at the Dolmetscher Institut der Universität Heidelberg we used to deal with almost correct texts in all combinations of our 3 languages.

With respect to this quality assessments (i.e. almost correct source texts), our teachers frequently used texts from the press, which they revised to the best of their knowledge and purpose. Teachers were preferentially looking for the output, we, on the other hand, were first looking for the quality of the texts to be translated. It was out of the question that we took for granted the quality of the source text.

The nature of such texts was informative and always referred to the technical field of our education (i.e. economics, jurisprudence, engineering, etc.). Literary texts were not the main goal of our education.

We believed that source text defects would impair good translations. That's why we took care to analyse the source text in the pre-translation phase. This was no common state-of-the-art in the linguistic field at that time. Doing this, we made the source text ready for better translation because we prevented errors before they arose. This translatability assessment was our quality control to guarantee that the source text was up to standards and didn't contain any errors in language related mistakes or alternative facts. At that point, after revision, the source text was in fact translatable.

| 1 | Definition: Translatability Assessment |
|---|---|
| The evaluation of the extent to which a measure [source text] can be meaningfully translated into another language.<br>Meaningful translation means that the translated text is conceptually equivalent to the source text. | |
| Source: Conway, K and Patrick, D. Translatability Assessment, in: C. Acquadro, K. Conway, C. Giroudet and I. Mear (Eds.), Linguistic validation manual for health outcome assessments, 2012, 127-132. | |
| A tried and tested method to optimize the master version of your assessment or survey questionnaire [source text] before the actual translation and adaption process begins. | |
| Source: Steve Dept, Mrielle Lerner, On Demand Webinar, Translatability Assessment, in: Survey translation and localisation, Test translation and localisation. | |

Nobody told us that. The intuitive understanding of both lexical and sentential relationships was in this actionable feedback context our modus operandi.

| 1 | Definition: Translation Assessment |
|---|---|
| Is a structured process that allows you to verify the quality of a translation.<br>In many respects, translation assessment aligns with quality assurance. | |
| Source: Web, OneSky, Translation Assessment: How to review Foreign-Language Content. | |

We usually found the mistakes and weak points in the texts and, day after day, we had fierce discussions with the teachers. Our translatability assessments could comprehend the faculty to identify errors in grammar, punctuation, logic, etc. The faculty to clear obscurities in words and wordings. The faculty to avoid interferences in the meaning of a whole sentence. The faculty to solve possible errors in the meta-language level of the message.

As a result, our translations were sometimes better than the first originals (the first original became more translatable in its revised version), even though our teachers cursed us during such classes.

Years later, during my excursions to the Dolmetscher Institut as a teacher, I always presented texts from real life to my students. That meant, source texts were unwashed, so they could learn how to deal in real life with real texts. They also had to develop a sense of evaluation. That meant, to evaluate how probable was that their supposition was correct? It also meant to find the author of the source text and how to address him with a concise question to get a satisfying answer.

Why a satisfying answer? Because the translator tries to identify errors, obscurities, interferences and more in the source text and needs the help of the responsible author/writer.

Fact is, on the other hand, that many source texts are written by writers with no education in professional writing for different countries. Frequently, company employees in a certain department are assigned (qualifications are not demanded) such tasks, just like that. That means, they are not technical writers and the source text English may already be a translation from a different language or this source text English is created by a non-native speaker with a deficient proficiency in English. As the saying goes: A little knowledge can be a dangerous thing.

In other words, the author/writer not necessarily knows the standards or norms to be observed in the technical documentation for country A or B or C. Nor does he know that the directive for the US-market is different from the directive for the European market. Therefore, adaptions from the relay language (mostly English, international as lingua franca) to the specific target country (USA, England, Ireland, Australia, etc.) must be done. The same procedure is to be observed by the other languages/countries. JP-, US- and EU-standards are not necessarily equivalent. The information or instruction may be correct, but the layout and wording standard can be false.

Depending on the author's/writer's mentality, the translator proceeds (should proceed) in different ways. If the author/writer has an Asian mentality the European translator has to compose his question in a different way as if he is addressing a Western author/writer. Consults via translation initiators or others in between can lead to the well-known Chinese whispers effect.

In this context, I can testify that real life texts are rarely impeccable, sometimes of poor quality and that the authors/writers selected not always appreciate linguistic corrections, objections and/or complaints (the template can be reduced to something like "everyone knows what is meant, so there is no necessity to correct my wording" meaning "stop annoying me!").

The aim of my classes was to state the source text quality defects in it and explain the potential strategies graduates may adopt when facing such texts. They had to identify any not fully understood term, and any term requiring further explanation, and any ambiguity with its options.

Finally, they listed without extra invitation all terminology and phraseology they considered important, including the research of equivalents. This terminology had, of course, to be validated in file and checked in consistency. This step was taken in team work.

## 1.1  Some Terms

Back to my students, in legal texts frequently appear terms that have to be explained and understood before translating. Fundamental terms like <Apostille>, <hipoteca>, <VAT Registration Number> or the equivalents or not-equivalents in the other languages.

Concerning the well-known <Apostille (Convention de La Haye du 5 octobre 1961)>, my predecessor in office, a lawyer, was not able to explain to my students during a whole semester what it is, how many points it includes or how it looks like.

| 1. | Elements of the Apostille |
| --- | --- |

Apostille
(Convention de La Haye du 5 octobre 1961)

1. Country: [county of issue]
This public document
2. has been signed by [who has signed the document]
3. acting in the capacity of [the capacity in which the person signed the document]
4. bears the seal/stamp of [details of any seal on the document]
Certified
5. at [place of issue]
6. the [date of issue]
7. by [issuing authority]
8. No. [Apostille Certificate number]
9. Seal/Stamp [seal of issuing authority]
10. Signature [signature of representative of issuing authority]

Layout can vary and be issued in one or more languages
Own source

In other words, the <Apostille> is a certification provided under the Hague Convention of 1961 for authenticating documents for use in foreign countries. It can be used only between countries which are members of this multilateral convention. Each member country determines which authorities are responsible for issuing the <Apostille>. The term could be cleared for the audience in 5 minutes.

Concerning <hipoteca> in the sentence <inmueble libre de hipotecas> in land register office's records, it appeared that my students were not able to understand the meaning of the term due to a lack of knowledge in this field.

| 1. | Definition: Hipoteca = Hypothek = Mortgage |
| --- | --- |

A legal agreement by which a bank, building society, etc. <u>lends</u> money at interest in exchange for taking title of the debtor's property, with the condition that the conveyance of title becomes void upon the payment of the debt.

Example: "I put down a hundred thousand in cash and took out a mortgage for the rest"

Source: Oxford languages, internet.
The meaning in Spanish, English and German is congruent.

They finally understood, after a large explanation and discussion, that a mortgage is a loan used to purchase or maintain a home, plot of land, or other real estate. The borrower agrees to pay the lender over time. In other words, it is a security someone gives for the money he gets from someone else for the purposes above specified.

Concerning <VAT Registration Number> in the European Union business fields, we had as of reference date 2010 according to the European Regulations a concordance for all country members, which was not accepted in Spain. That's why in Spanish texts a lot of variants were and are still found for the term.

| 1. | VAT Term: Concordance in 5 European countries | |
|---|---|---|
| County | Term in the official language | Abbreviation |
| Germany | Umsatzsteuer-Identifikationsnummer | USt-IdNr. |
| Ireland Éire | VAT identification number | VAT No. |
| Austria | Umsatzsteuer-Identifikationsnummer | UID-Nr. |
| Spain | Número de identificación a efectos del impuesto del Valor Añadido | N.IVA |
| United Kingdom | VAT registration number | VAT Reg. No. |
| Source: Bundeszentralamt für Steuern as of reference date 2010. | | |

The long and the short of it is that in Spain authorities don't give one official term for this kind of tax. Terms mostly used in Spain are: <Número de Identificación del Impuesto sobre el Valor Añadido> and <Número de Identificación del Impuesto al Valor Agregado>, but not exclusively. The same happens with the abbreviation. In this context, the cherry on the cake is that the <número de indentificación fiscal (NIF)> (= <tax number>) is also used in variations like <N.IVA> and similars, and sometimes <NIF> as generic for both tax types.

| 1. | Documentation: N.IVA |
|---|---|
| Notas marginales [en una inscripción de un catastro]:<br>Esta finca queda afectada al pago de impuestos y derechos que indica la nota al margen de la inscripción extensa que en la adjunta se expresa.<br>Los derechos incluyen el IVA especificado debiendo el destinatario indicar su número de identificación fiscal para efectos del impuesto al valor agregado (N.IVA).<br>Cancelada la anterior nota, ****((ciudad))***, a ***((fecha))***<br>((firma: ilegible)) | |
| Own source from 1993 | |

In this document, N.IVA is used in the meaning of VAT registration number.

| 1. | Documentation: NIF = N.IVA |
| --- | --- |

Notas marginales [en una inscripción de un catastro]:
Esta finca queda afectada al pago de impuestos y derechos que indica la nota al margen de la inscripción extensa que en la adjunta se expresa.
Los derechos incluyen el IVA especificado debiendo el destinatario indicar su número de identificación fiscal para efectos del impuesto sobre el valor añadido (NIF).
Cancelada la anterior nota, ****((ciudad))***, a ***((fecha))***
((firma: ilegible))

Own source from 1993

In this similar document, NIF is used in the meaning of VAT registration number.

In both cases the documents are issued in the same city by the same land registry office in Spain, both in 1993.Long Live the Mayhem!

## 1.2 Some Wordings

In the legal field, professionals have the urge to express a fact or action or whatever in a very peculiar way. The following examples may help to understand what I mean.

| 1.2 | Example 1: Wording in German |
| --- | --- |
| Public prosecutor:<br>XYZ wird wegen Totschlags zum Nachteil seiner Frau angeklagt | |

Own source

As a brain teaser, the reader may try to "translate" the sentence into his working languages. In this case, the meaning is "XYZ wird wegen Totschlags an seiner Frau angeklagt" (that means something like "XYZ is charged with the/accused of manslaughter of his wife"). In any case, the meaning here is important and also the difference between murder, homicide, manslaughter, assassination. Remember: we dive into German Law. English and Spanish have a different approach.

| 1.2 | Example 2: Wording in German/German and Swiss/German |
| --- | --- |
| Court sentence:<br>(Germany:)<br>die Kosten des Rechtsstreits werden gegeneinander aufgehoben<br>(Switzerland:)<br>die Parteikosten werden wettgeschlagen | |

Own source

We concentrate on German Law: The Code of Civil Procedure, Section 92 (1) says in the official Ministery English translation (look for <(German) code of civil procedure> on the web): "If the costs have been cancelled against each other, the parties shall bear the court costs at one half each". In Spanish it would be approx.: <las partes procesales sufragan por mitad las tasas judiciales y costean c/u de ellas sus propios gastos extrajudiciales>. Now, it is up to the reader to adapt the text to a specific translation/language.

In Switzerland, according to the Code of Civil Procedure, <Wettschlagen> means, <dass jede Partei ihre eigenen Kosten, insbesondere ihre notwendigen Auslagen wie Anwaltskosten selber trägt und die Gerichtskosten geteilt werden>. That means, both wordings/terms are in this case equivalent.

In such cases, the linguist expert must be able to immediately comprehend the source text/oral statement in order to translate/interpret the message the right way.

# 1.3 Background of the Translator

The translator can have an educational background at the university or not. The university background means completing the education with a degree (BA, MA or else) at an institute of the university. Another background can be obtained at other schools, commercial chambers, basic secondary/grade/senior schools, professional associations/entities or else. In the latter case, the term <certified> frequently used in English leads to misunderstandings.

In abstract terms, linguists (that means translators and interpreters) differ from each other in many ways mainly due to their knowledge and professional conditions (meaning background). The combination of all individual differences and characteristics of a subject may directly influence the output (translation/interpreting) quality.

In the technical field, there is a great need for competent linguists, and a great need of the outposters to minimize the cost factor. This simply leads to mediocrity and is an ignored point in linguistic (translation/interpreting) studies.

In this context, in the past not many studies have directly examined the relationship between individuals' level of education and their job performance.

The years of work experience do not necessarily moderate the education-performance relationship because work experience often only indicates the quantity not the quality of the output (the well-known phrase of applicants for a job: "I can translate 5000 words/day", no matter in which technical field).

Of course, some dimensions of performance are influenced by education. For instance, professional linguists without an academic degree in this field do not necessarily focus on the revision stage. This can challenge the quality of the output; but also, it can mean that qualified linguists and academics recognize the significance of this factor.

I think, the academic status of the linguist should be taken into account as one of the elements of his/her sense of responsibility which undoubtedly influences the process and the quality of his/her output.

A linguist is expected to have good knowledge in a great number of fields to perform a better job. While people tend to specialize in few and narrow areas, linguists are expected to have a very good knowledge of all the domains they think they might need. That is why translation/interpreting students expect to receive solid and complex training which allows them to face the challenges of translating/interpreting in real life situations. Most of the students expect their teachers to give them the opportunity to acquire profound knowledge and skills in many areas associated with their future profession.

| See | Luis R. Cerna: CVs and Freelancers. Norderstedt 2024. ISBN 976-3-7597-4896-6 |
|---|---|

### 1.3.1 University Background

The university degree implies a solid education at high level. The degree is granted not because the student knows everything, but because he knows how to scientifically investigate/penetrate a new operational field.

At the university the translator in spe learns by lectures, seminars and exercises, exercises, exercises and more exercises how to manage specific texts. Mostly, the translator in spe selects as his technical expertise/subject the courses offered for this purpose in the faculties of Economics, Jurisprudence or in any other university faculty.

To put it clearly, the standard university formation requires courses and the correspondent exams in one native language, two foreign languages and one technical expertise/subject.

The translator in spe must have an affinity to process conducting research. Research skills encompass a very important trait any translator should have; that is to say, curiosity.

The importance of research is crucial for the translator in spe and the university allows him an access into the new dry matter, in which he will need to acquire first knowledge (a new expertise field) as employee or freelancer.

Why a new field? Because the translator in spe cannot know or expect to get jobs in the fields he has already dug into. Junior translators, both employees or freelancers, face as starters the challenge of market offers. They cannot select the jobs they want to do. They must earn money to survive and pay their bills. They must take what comes and be able to complete the assigned work. For this goal they must be realistic, prudent, smart, and open minded.

To excel in the field of translations, the translator in spe needs a robust blend of skills. Firstly, a strong grasp of both the source and target languages is fundamental. But beyond linguistic prowess, the translator must deeply understand the technical field he is translating, whether it's medical, legal, engineering, or else. Familiarity with industry-specific terminology and concepts is crucial. Precision and attention to detail are paramount, as even a minor error can alter the meaning significantly. Adaptability is also a key, as he'll often navigate between different formats and styles. Effective research skills help in staying updated with industry developments.

On the one hand, technical translation is the process of transferring the meaning of a technical text from one language to another. This requires scientific, technical industrial knowledge, proficiency in the use of technical terminology and jargon in both the source and target language, and the ability to transpose concepts with precision.

On the other hand, in legal translation, research skills are crucial, particularly for comparative law research (Roman, Anglo-Saxon law, etc.). It's not just about finding language equivalents, but understanding how legal concepts vary across jurisdictions. A lawyer linguist, will always emphasize the importance of accurately verifying terms and their context in different legal systems. Utilizing diverse resources like legal databases, search engines, and academic journals is the key. This, combined with critical thinking and analysis, ensures translations, which are linguistically precise and legally coherent, respecting the nuances of each legal culture/system.

One last example for the field of medical translators: No one will deny that it's very important and very critical to have a medical background in this field. It helps in the translation of medical texts if the translator works precisely and professionally. A wrong translation of any medical terminology can generate a life-threatening condition. To put it in medical terms, any gain of experience and any feedback in this field is a plus, and remember that translation just like muscles need to be trained every day

Domain expertise is non-negotiable in the translation field. The same happens with deep industry knowledge. The university background helps translators in spe to obtain a solid basis to start their careers. No more, no less.

## 1.3.2 Other Backgrounds

While formal qualifications are not always mandatory in the world, having advanced multilingual skills (bilingual is not enough) or a BA, MA or another university degree in Interpreting and Translation Sciences is advantageous. Additionally, the translator must demonstrate language proficiency, ethical competence, and intercultural competence. It's also beneficial to join industry associations for support, professional development, and networking opportunities. It is better to complete any formal training below university level and meet certain prerequisites.

There are so many possibilities as countries in the world to obtain a certificate (below graduate level) for the profession. Don't mix the terms <certificate for the profession>, i.e. <certified translator> and <the faculty (translator's certification at court) to issue certified translations for official use in a country>, i.e. <certified translator>.

| 1.3.2 | Homonym <certified translator> |
| --- | --- |
| First acception | Translator with a certificate for the translator*s profession (below graduate level). |
| Second acception | Translator with the faculty/license to issue certified translations for official use in a country (i.e. translator's certification at court). |

Homonym = Each of two or more words having the same spelling and pronunciation but different meanings.
Own source

Some countries use the term <certified translator> for a translator with a certification to practice the profession issued by a national recognized entity other than universities. Some other countries use the term <certified translator> for a translator, which has been sworn at the corresponding court (in Germany the competent Regional Court of the professional domicile of the applicant) with the faculty to issue <certified translations> (vulgo: <sworn translations>) for official use in the country (the use outside of this country must be additionally legalized by a Apostille if both, the source and target country, have accepted (are members of) the "Convention de La Haye du 5 octobre 1961"). Otherwise, a different routine applies (commonly: mandatory double legalisation).

The explanation above is an excellent example for deathly antonyms in the linguistic branch. For the US linguist and the German linguist, the same word may imply different concepts and they are not necessarily aware of the misunderstanding in their conversation/interchange/dialogue, or worst, monologue.

In the best case, the misunderstanding may sooner or later be clarified.

Back to the USA: The National Accreditation Authority for Translators and Interpreters (NAATI), for example, requires different levels of training depending on the type of credential the candidate is seeking. This candidate has only the minimum certification of been fluent in a first and second language. In this case, language knowledge in two languages is a fundamental requirement for becoming a certified translator.

Getting certified in the USA, i.e. getting a certificate for the profession, is a valuable step for translators without university degrees. While not obligatory, it enhances the credibility and showcases the expertise of the translator:

In the US: The American Translators Association (ATA) exam covers general, legal, and medical translation.

In the UK: The Chartered Institute of Linguists (CIOL) offers certifications in various levels and fields.

For other countries, the candidate should look for certifications from regional or international organizations relevant to his language pair or specialization. Each has unique criteria, so the candidate can select one that aligns with his skills and career aspirations.

Certifications not only validate the translator's proficiency but also open new professional avenues if wisely used.

### 1.3.3 Self-taught Background

Most people think translation is all about knowing a second language. But it's more about knowing a target language, which is in many cases the mother tongue of the candidate. That's the first step in the linguistic profession. There is a point at the candidate's journey that he realizes how poor his mother tongue and first foreign language skills are. He feels the urge to read great literature in his working languages, writing down words, and start looking for the origin of words. Etymology means having knowledge in at least Latin and Old Greek, but also first documentation of a word can sometimes be meaningful. This is the point where translation begins. Before this, the candidate is just putting meaningless words together.

The first thing that a candidate needs if he wants to be a good translator is to be fully fluent in two languages. The phantom statement that good translators only translate into the language that is native to them is a fairy tale. Good translators translate from three into two languages. This is because even if the candidate has a great understanding of a foreign language, most people struggle to write with grammatical accuracy in a foreign language. In this context, the linguistic mentality achieved in one person is not a one but a two ways street.

The self-taught background is the way per aspera ad astra. The candidate must invent the wheel again and again because he has not the introductory patterns of a formal education offered by a university or other entities. He must be simultaneously teacher and pupil. At the end, the victorious candidate is per se a good translator and manages later to obtain a certification for the profession. Then the job is done!

## 1.3.4 Proofreading and Tools

The proofreading process for quality assurance, helping tools like translation quality assessment models, glossaries and machine translation programs are herein not taken into consideration.

The focus of this publication is the best possible overview of the source texts (situation) as they reach the linguistic experts and how the linguistic experts proceed in translating and fixing deficient texts.

Quality is more than the sum of its parts and the identification of translation problems is essential for the adequate solution of such problems.

# 2. The Situation

In linguistic environments, the question of quality is almost exclusively related to that of the target language. Hereinafter, the quality of both, source and target language, and their interactions are stated and evaluated.

Most publications in the branch take for granted that the source text (also when it acts like a relais for other languages, i.e. when it is not the real source text) for a translation is impeccable. This is not always the case as already explained.

In this case, the linguistic expert has the option between a) to correct the translation (the source text is corrected in the translation without changing the manuscript) without notification of the outsourcer and b) to correct the source text telling the outsourcer the changes.

Case a) means the errors in the source text remain. Some translations in other languages may keep the mistakes when the other translators don't proceed as the first translator and fix the errors without saying a word.

The case of one translator proceeding this way is documented.

| 2. | Correcting the source text without notification of the outsourcer |
|---|---|
| The translator makes the experience that the outsourcer is unable to accept that he makes mistakes.<br>The translator corrects mentally the source text without making changes in the source text and doesn't tell the outsourcer the found mistakes.<br>The translator is unhappy and after a while he finishes the cooperation. | |
| Own source. | |

The situation is intolerable for the linguistic expert and infertile for all parties. Corpses are dragged along (from the uncorrected source language English into the other target languages).

Case b) means the outsourcer is notified, accept the changes and re-edit the source text ("extra charge" for the outsourcer). The translation into other languages avoids the transport of errors (no corpses are dragged along).

| 2. | Correcting the source text with notification of the outsourcer |
|---|---|
| The translator makes the experience that the outsourcer is willing to accept that he makes mistakes.<br>The translator corrects mentally the source text, makes changes in the source text and notifies the outsourcer about the mistakes he found.<br>The outsourcer revises the source text and issues the proofread text.<br>The translator is happy. | |
| Own source. | |

This is a win-win situation for all parties. The outsourcer can now be sure that mistakes were deleted and his good image among his clients improves (collateral benefit as an interceding good fortune). The linguistic expert knows his expertise is welcome.

| See | Luis R. Cerna: CVs and Freelancers. Norderstedt 2024. ISBN 976-3-7597-4896-6. Point 4.1 Hourly rate. |
| --- | --- |

Now, let's have a look at the term <impeccable>:

| 2. | Definition: Word Family <impeccable> |
| --- | --- |
| Merrian-Webster defines the word family <impeccable> as follows:<br>The word *impeccable* has been used in English since the 16th century. It comes from the Latin word *impeccabilis*, a combination of the Latin prefix *in-*, meaning "not," and the verb *peccare*, meaning "to sin." Its original meaning hewed close to its root: *impeccable* meant "not capable of sinning or liable to sin." (It has a rare but pleasingly logical antonym in *peccable*, meaning "liable or prone to sin.") *Peccare* has other descendants in English: there is the noun *peccadillo*, ("a slight offense"), adjective *peccant* ("guilty of a moral offense" or simply "faulty"), and the noun *peccavi*, which in Latin literally means "I have sinned" but in English refers to an acknowledgment of sin. Nowadays, *impeccable* is more commonly used in the secular sense to mean "flawless," as in "impeccable taste in music" or "their craftsmanship is impeccable." |

Source: Merriam Webster, internet.

If the source text is correct as specified, we don't have to analyze it after checking it. Keep in mind, during the translation process the translator analyzes one more time the source text and the proofreader analyzes one more time the translated text. If the text is still correct, somebody did a great job and that's it!

Some other times, the source text can be correct, but useless ("nice but hopeless") when the standards (norms) are not observed or the linguistic reflection, meaning the perspective, is not adapted.

| 2. | Case 1: Standards and linguistic reflection perspective not observed |
| --- | --- |
| Ms. (draft) | Always turn off the power and unplug the machine, then only authorized technicians are allowed to change the specifications for *** to that for ***. |
| Revised | Authorized technicians only.<br>Before starting turn off the power.<br>Unplug the machine.<br>Change the specifications for *** to that for ***.<br>Plug in the machine.<br>Turn off the power.<br>Check the change. |

Own source

The original text of Case 1 was written in a very polite Asian language and translated "as seen" into English as relais language for other languages. The result may sound very polite, be accurate and correct in the original language, but in English (relais source text) and other languages it is only confusing.

The goal is to guide the authorized technician step by step in a clear and unequivocal way during a change of specifications/settings (activity) in a machine (see revised version on the Table above).

Next step is to adapt (if necessary) the text to the standards valid for the target country/zone (USA, Europe, etc.). This rewriting is essential for bad texts and texts written outside of the norm required for a specific country. Doing this, errors can be prevented before they arise.

Comparing the target text to the source text checking if the target text is a true, accurate, precise, correct, quantitative and qualitative reproduction of the source text is not enough. The complex phenomenon of translation is more.

That means, the standard procedure should be
1. To translate the manuscript draft into clear English.
2. To adapt/transcreate the clear version to the target language English.
3. To adapt the cleared version to the target standards/norms for the target country/zone.

As already stated, English acts sometimes as relais for other languages. For example, when the original source language is a rare language or when the source language has a different perspective or approach to the target audience. In this case, the same procedure starts again for the next language.

In a first step, the translator translates as indicated in the Table of Case 1, line <Ms. (draft)>. He delivers the translation with a corresponding remark to the outsourcer.

In a second step, the outsourcer decides what to do. If a revision/adaptation is desired, the outsourcer appoints a translator or technician or both to do the job.

In a third step, the outsourcer appoints the translator, technician, or technical writer to adapt the text to the norms valid for the target country (English can be used for the Australian, Canadian, GB, Irish, US, etc. market).

The idea that the translator should do all this for the originally agreed translation fee is starry-eyed. It means for the translator to invest unpaid time for undesired high quality according to the legal norm.

On the other hand, some outsourcers want to deskill the task looking for so-called acceptable output (not clear instructions for use) in terms of poor quality in the linguistic industry. In this case, a decent reference to product liability laws may be highly appreciated and understood by wise outsourcers (see point 3). A "good translation" is not always good enough. The assessment criteria depend on the purpose of the text. Different ideas of "what a good translation is" lead to different evaluations of the translational quality. Instructions must simultaneously keep in mind the legal and technical aspect of each text in each language.

## 2.1 Services Free of Charge

When a physician tries to impose his standards for invoicing industrial technique services, the result will be as expected because he is hunting (by trespassing) in someone else's territory.

When the development and research division tries to impose its standards for invoicing linguistic services, the result will be as expected, because it is hunting (by trespassing) in someone else's territory.

When the linguistic division tries to impose its standards for not invoicing editing services, the result will be as expected, because it is hunting (by trespassing) in someone else's territory.

When the translator desists of charging for (re-)editing services, the result for the translator will be as expected, because the same translator is hunting (by trespassing) in someone else's territory.

Of course, any text must be understood before translating into another language, but if the text is not clear enough and must be re-edited in cooperation with the translator, this kind of service must be accordingly remunerated, because the translator invests extra time in this (re-)editing, not translating process.

The core message is that the translator doesn't only translate words and grammatical structures, but texts as communicative messages.

In the following, the perspective of some translators will be pointed out.

| 2.1 | Example: Translator 1 |
|---|---|
| If the materials have conflicted content, I review related documents and working communication to see the connections so I would know the full context. And I consult the technical expert on the area of the document. This technical expert might not have language skills, but based on the context, he can offer advises on the right direction. | |
| Source: Web | |

If the material has conflicted content, and these texts fulfill a specific function, it means re-editing is necessary. This is an additional step not included in the translation process and should be correspondingly remunerated.

| 2.1 | Example: Translator 2 |
|---|---|
| I cross-check the sources, that means, I compare the translation with the original text for discrepancies. | |
| Source: Web | |

Cross-checking source and target texts is state of the art in the translation process. This proofreading is part of the translation process. The specific internal and external characteristics of a specific technical text are conventionalized. Any re-editing of the source/target text due to conflicts found by means of the translation is extra work and should be correspondingly remunerated.

| 2.1 | Example: Translator 3 |
| --- | --- |
| If the materials have conflicted content, I consult bilingual experts for their insights. | |
| Source: Web | |

User manuals are highly conventionalized text types at all levels. Even if the expert belongs to my client's company, his time costs money to the company. The same applies to my time and therefore it is legitimate to charge for the time of the consultation. If the expert doesn't belong to my client's company, higher fees for his time also apply.

To make it clear in this context, the reflection of some translators, these services are part of the translation and they are already included in the translation fee is false. This is an extra service that should be correspondingly remunerated.

| 2.1 | Example: Translator 4 |
| --- | --- |
| A translation specialist is like a linguistic superhero, swooping in to save the day when language barriers threaten to wreak havoc! Picture them with a cape made of dictionaries, armed with a keyboard and a mighty pen, ready to tackle any linguistic challenge. Their mission? To bridge the gap between languages with the finesse of a tightrope walker – ensuring that jokes don't turn into awkward silences and that puns maintain their pun-iness. They're the unsung heroes making sure your favorite punchline in one language doesn't become a confusing head-scratcher in another. Think of them as language acrobats, flipping and somersaulting through idioms all while keeping the essence of the original message intact. | |
| Source: Web | |

Well, it may be all that and more, depending on text, author, and target audience. The typological conventions in the source/target language and culture and the communicative situation are to be observed. The wording for the instructions for the use of a device is differently structured than the wording for the instructions for assembling a desk or the wording for a patent application in the chemical or mechanical or other industry and should be correspondingly remunerated.

| 2.1 | Example: Translator 5 |
| --- | --- |
| I would add that having knowledge about design helps. Of course, it doesn't mean a translator should design the documents, since that's the job of designers, but knowing the basics is a plus to understand what a complete project requires, from the perspective of some clients. | |
| Source: Web | |

Design considerations are important aspects and extra work, and this knowledge needs a supplementary remuneration for the translator. To put hands on a text and to make suggestions to improve the source/target text means re-editing and the extra service should be correspondingly remunerated.

| 2.1 | Example: Translator 6 |
| --- | --- |
| Nowadays, it is essential to be able to reuse translated content. This is made possible by CAT tools. These tools also make it possible to 1) perform a series of almost automatic quality checks 2) ensure terminology consistency by using and creating terminology databases 3) work with file types that would otherwise be very difficult or impossible to translate (InDesign, Json, html, xml, etc.) 4) keep reference files "handy" for quick consultation. | |
| Source: Web | |

Any extra work or knowledge needs a supplementary remuneration for the translator. The linguistic models concerning fees have changed and such evolutions should not be detrimental to the linguistic expert. Machines and programs for automatically quality checks, to ensure terminology consistency, to transcribe types and to keep reference files handy in order to improve the source/target text always means re-editing and the extra service should be correspondingly remunerated.

A good translation is not only the reproduction of the source text, it is a functionally appropriate translation of the message given by the source text.

## 2.2 Examples for Bad Instructions

The translation quality may be a central issue in the target text evaluation, but the source text quality is essential for a good translation.

In this context, please keep in mind that certified translations are a big exception: The certified translation of official documents (like birth certificates, etc.) doesn't allow changes or correction of any kind. A certified translation is an official translation made by a translator, sworn at the corresponding court, empowered to certify translations for official purposes.

In all other cases, bad instruction can mean: a) The source text is perfect and the translation is deficient. b) The source text is deficient and the translation too. c) The source text is deficient and the translation is perfect.

When the source text is perfect and the translation deficient, this means the translation is bad, the outsourcer should reject the work after proofreading, demand corrections and revise the corrected text again. If the translation is good, the outsourcer accepts the corrected/amended translation and that's it.

When the source text is deficient and the translation too, this means both parties must find a modus vivendi (if not already specified in the contractual terms). The standard procedure for a good translator is to point out the bad quality of the source text (specifying, if possible, the weak points) before delivering the translation. The delivery of a bad translation (without saying a word) of a bad source text is unusual.

When the source text is deficient and the translation perfect, this means the translator may have specified the weak points in the source text or not. If he doesn't specify the weak points, the source text remains unchanged (normally, translators have no access to the master file of the manuscript). In other cases, the parties proceed according to the contractual terms or make a posterior agreement on this point.

Source text deficiencies can occur when the source text has wrong interpunction, misspellings, omissions, was not written by a native speaker or equivalent, was not written by a technical writer or equivalent, doesn't fulfill the directive/standard prescribed for a country/zone, doesn't specify the target directive/standard to be observed for a specific country to replace the original directive/standard in the source text, the correspondence between menu options in texts and display options is not given, etc.

The decisive fact is to know the purpose of the text (what texts are supposed to be used for) and how the effects are achieved. In other words, the linguistic expert must know what the users want to do with the text (action to be guided by instructions, etc.).

In the daily world of technology there is an increasing volume of instructions for the use of all kind of devices to be translated.

Let us analyze the standard procedure in a specific case (with happy ending):
Responsible purchaser of the translations: R+D Department, company X (a)
Distributor: Linguistic Department, same company X (b)
Contractor: Freelancers (linguistic experts) for the different translations (c, d, e…).

The responsible purchaser (a) sends a purchase order to the distributor (b) and the distributor distributes the source text among the linguistic experts (c, d, e...) responsible for the different target languages. The finished translation is returned in reverse order to the responsible purchaser (a). The manuals are printed and distributed with the devices to the customers.

The Purchase Order (PO) is essential for the output and for company X and always looks like the following template (in our case).

| 2.2. | Purchase Order, Company X |
|---|---|
| Please find attached source text (English) to be translated into (German, Spanish, French ...). (Additional information, if any) Due date **/**/****. | |

Own source

No restrictions or further specifications for the functional approach were stated herein and the source text was translated as specified in the PO.

In this case, it was a user manual to be translated into German, Spanish, and French. The manual contained machine setting instructions and options to select on a display.

| 2.2. | Example 1: User Manual (machine setting instructions, extract) |
|---|---|
| Touch the "Setting Function" key. On this screen, you can select either "ON" or "OFF" for "Auto Presser Foot Lift", "Finger (Chain Stitch) (retractable chaining-off finger for thread chain)" or "Auto Stop (Easy Display) (automatic stop of plain seaming)". | |

Own source

Linguistic experts translated the whole text into the target languages as specified in the purchase order. The manuals were printed and delivered with the device. The customers in the target languages complained that they couldn't use the instructions because the "screens" showed only English text and the instructions text was in the corresponding customer's target language. There was no concordance between display and instructions. The manufacturer had to revise (post-editing work for the linguistic experts and others, extra-paid), reprint and redistribute the manual. A certain image loss couldn't be avoided.

After the necessary general revision, the instructions were "functional" and the costumers received the amended version with nice apologies for the inconvenience and were satisfied with an appropriate deduction.

By mass products, the above indicated solution is usually never practiced. The customer has to solve the problem by himself and a loss of reputation doesn't really count for the manufacturer.

| 2.2. | Example 2: Time setting of a clock (user manual in German) |
| --- | --- |
| Zeiteinstellung<br>   1.  Wählen Sie mit den Tasten >/< (vor/zurück) die Menüoption "Zeiteinstellung" aus und bestätigen Sie mit SELECT.<br>   2.  Wählen Sie mit den Tasten >/< (vor/zurück) das gewünschte Untermenü auf:<br>Zeiteinstellung: manuelle Zeit- und Datumeinstellung<br>Uhrformat: Auswahl zwischen 12/24 Stundenformat<br>Auto update: Auswahl zwischen DAB Update, FM Update, Any Update oder No Update | |

Own source

The menu option "Zeiteinstellung" didn't exist (the name of the menu option was "Time setup" in English). "Uhrformat" didn't exist (the name of the menu option was "Clock format" in English). This user manual was deficient for the German market. Customers with English knowledge could easily solve the problem reading the English instructions, but that is not the point! The instructions were "unfunctional".

Such deficiencies happen when the purchaser orders the translation without further specifications for the functional approach. The (German) buyer was not able to set the clock according to the delivered (German) instructions.

| 2.2. | Example 3: Motorhaube öffnen (user manual in German) |
| --- | --- |
| Entriegeln des Sicherheitshakens der Fronthaube<br>Ziehen Sie zum Entriegeln der Motorhaube den Sicherheitshaken ein wenig nach oben und bewegen Sie die Lasche 4 in Pfeilrichtung A, um den Haken 2 zu lösen). | |

Own source

The instruction and the corresponding Figure in the user manual of the car are confusing, no concordant and don't allow to fulfill the aimed task. The user cannot open the engine hood following the German instructions and is mostly desperate in such cases. The instructions are "unfunctional". The user feels not being taken seriously. The private instruction and corresponding video on the web are, on the contrary, excellent. The user feels being taken seriously by a fellow in misery.

A good instruction could be: Lift the hood a little so you can introduce your hand between car body and hood. Move your hand until you feel the safety hood. At its right you feel under your fingers the blocking latch. Press this down and lift the hood all the way up…

It is inconceivable to any user why the original instruction is like that.

Example for bad English:

| 2.2. | Example 4: ...will be turned on the operation panel... |
|---|---|
| Sensor ON/OFF setting:<br>Function setting xxx: In the case the front/intermediate/rear sensor is set to "ON" with this function setting number, LED (B/C/D) will be turned on the operation panel when the front/intermediate/rear sensor detects the material. | |



The wording <will be turned on the operation panel> is bad English. English demands here <on> two times and the active is better than the passive voice, that means the wording was corrected as suggested by the translator: <...will turn on on the operation panel...>.

Bad instructions or information also occur when the wrong term is used.

| 2.2. | Example 5: Occurrence |
|---|---|
| Occurrence:<br>Vitamin A (Retinol) occurs only in feed components of animal origin such as fish lever oil, milk, fish meal etc. Feeds of plant origin contain only various provitamins, the carotenoids. Of the total carotenes, beta-carotene usually constitutes more than 90%. All green plants and carrots are rich in beta-carotene, whereas all other plant products like grain, potatoes, beets etc., with the exception of corn grain, contains little or no carotene. [...]<br><br>Ocurrencia:<br>La vitamina A (retinol) se halla solamente en piensos de origen animal, como aceite de higado de pez, leche, harina de pez, etc. En los piensos vegetales solo se encuentran las previtaminas de la vitamina A, los carotenos. Aquí se encuentra el beta-caroteno en una proporción superior al 90%. Ricas en beta-caroteno son especialmente todas las plantas verdes y, entre las raíces, las zanahorias, mientras todos los demás productos vegetales, como los cereales, con excepción del maíz, patatas, remolachas, etc. y sus residuos de manipulación contienen poco o nada de caroteno. [...} | |



Considering <occurrence> and <ocurrencia> (think of the sentence: menuda ocurrencia sacar el paraguas en medio de una tormenta eléctrica) as equivalent is a canonical case of faux amis. In this case, <presencia> is the better option.

A lack of knowledge seduces the translator to use <pez> instead of <pescado>. The fundamental difference is that <pez> refers to the animal while it is alive in the water, <pescado> implies that the animal is already dead and can undergo further processing. It also applies to the processed (new) product (<harina de pescado>).

In the technical field, there is no reason to change <provitamins> into <previtaminas> because the standard term is <provitaminas>.

The use of <patatas> in a text for different countries is not the best option. It is correct for Spain but not for Latin America. The best option in this case is to use <papas/patatas>.

The information is "unfunctional".

One more wrong term in an instruction's manual.

| 2.2. | Example 6: Conduction parts = Transmission parts |
| --- | --- |
| The pulley, belt, parts around the thread take-up shaft that function as the thread take-up conduction parts are covered by the thread take-up shaft cover and the pully belt cover. These parts rotate during… | |
| Own source | |

The translator asked if the term <conduction parts> was a wrong term for <transmission parts>. The outsourcer confirmed this, and the wrong term could be corrected in the source text.

And now a short text of six words in English (product listing) with some mistakes.

| 2.2. | Example 7: Crop Protection |
| --- | --- |
| Crop protection: See herbicides, see fungicides, […]:<br><br>Protección de plantas: Véase herbicidas, véase fungicidas […] | |
| Own source (Technical leaflet) | |

The technical term for <crop protection-> is in Spanish <fitosanidad>, period. The reference <véase> is singular. When referring to more than one object, chapter, etc., is better to use <véanse>, that means plural.

The information is "unfunctional".

The lack of technical vocabulary is detrimental to a functional translation (instruction, information, message) in the industrial field. The associations which the use of the standard term implies are not given when a false term is used.

| 2.2. | Example 8: Vliesstoff – Nonwoven, Non-Woven – Tela(s) sin Tejer |
| --- | --- |
| German (source text):<br>Die Laminierung von Vliesstoffen mit Kunststoffschäumen führte 1963 zur Produktion von Feinsynthetiks.<br><br>Spanish (target text):<br>La laminación de vellones no tejidos con gomaespumas llevó en 1963 a la producción de materiales sintéticos finos. | |
| Own source (Technical leaflet) | |

The technical term for <Vliestoff> is in Spanish <tela(s) sin tejer>. In some companies however, the English influence reflects in the construction <no tejidos>.

<Kunststoffschäume> can be translated as <gomaespumas> and <espumas plásticas>. <führte> can be better translated as <permitió>.

The information is "unfunctional".

And now a similar mistake in a different context:

| 2.2. | Example 9: Spinnvlies(stoff) – Spunbonded Nonwoven – Tela sin Tejer de Filamento Continuo |
|---|---|
| English (source text):<br>Spunbonded nonwovens made by XXX are high-strength, fabric-like materials that are used in a large variety of applications all over the world.<br><br>Spanish (target text):<br>Los vellones sintejer de filamentos continuos producidos por XXX, son materiales de estructura similar al textil, extremadamente resistentes, utilizados en todo el mundo para multitud de usos. | |

Own source (Technical leaflet)

<Spunbonded nonwovens> are <telas sin tejer de filamento continuo>. <fabric-like materials> are <materiales de estructura casi textil>.

The information is "unfunctional".

A translated text is functional when it conforms to the conventions and norms ruling this concrete text type. Vocabulary can be part of these conventions and norms producing the linguistic and technical correctness of the (source and target) text.

The chemical conventions and norms demand the correct orthography (the conventional/standard spelling system to record something in writing) of sulfuric acid as chemical formula $H_2SO_4$ and not H2SO4 or $2\text{-}C_4H_3O$ (2-furyl = univalent radical derived from furan by removal of one hydrogen atom = the alpha or 2-radical) and not 2-C4H30 as some sales departments or marketing people (may) think.

The same happens when using the wrong technical term or wording as stated above. The wording <vellones no tejidos/sintejer> sounds good but isn't!

In this context, the translation quality is not per se given, it depends on the technical field, on the text creator (source texter and translator and proofreader), on the function (instructions, information, etc.) and on the text recipients. The information given to an engineer can be different from the one given to an operator or to a non-technical consumer.

To optimize the translation (target language version), the proofreader must at least have the same qualification as the translator. This is not always the case.

Last, but not least: a good solution doesn't have to be a translation. The film industry can be extremely creative as shown below.

| 2.2. | Example 10: R2-D2 (Star Wars) |
| --- | --- |
| English (source text):<br>R2-D2 [= the fictional robot character in the Star Wars]<br><br>Spanish LA (target text):<br>Arturito. | |

Own source (Film)

R2-D2 is called the same in many languages. In Latin America, however, it is called <Arturito>. Below the story as Spoiler (Web) says:

| 2.2. | The Story behind Arturito |
| --- | --- |
| Lo cierto es que **Arturito**, tal como lo conocemos en Latinoamérica, en realidad se llama **R2D2**, que en inglés se pronuncia *"artuditu"* y por eso los traductores de este lado del mundo aprovecharon el parecido de esa pronunciación con el simpático nombre que eligieron darle a un personaje que pasaría a la historia como uno de los grandes valores dentro de la mitología de **Star Wars**. ¡Fue propiedad tanto de Anakin Skywalker como de su hijo Luke! | |

Source: Spoiler (Web)
https://spoiler.bolavip.com/cine/reparto-de-blanca-nieves-y-el-cazador-en-netflix

In other words, the people responsible tried to come as close as possible to the English pronunciation of the robot name, and, indeed, R2-D2 sounds similar to Arturito when spoken out loud (remember: "R2"/"Artoo", sounds like "Arthur"). Another factor to keep in mind is that in Latin America most films are subtitled and not dubbed. The real reason for selecting Arturito will remain a mystery of "The Force".

In this context, it is interesting to know the story behind the English name R2-D2. The same source says:

| 2.2. | The Story behind R2-D2 |
| --- | --- |
| ¿Cómo llegó a llamarse **R2D2** este astrodroide? El nombre surgió durante el rodaje de la película *American Graffiti* de **George Lucas** que recordó: *"Una noche estábamos buscando el Rollo 2, Diálogo 2 de la película. De repente alguien gritó R2D2. A Walter Murch, que mezclaba la película y a mí nos gustó mucho ese nombre y nos quedamos con él"*. Claro, el emblemático cineasta ya se encontraba trabajando en lo que sería su mayor éxito y de ahí el nombre original para **Arturito**. | |



In other words, the name derives from a different context (Walter Murch and George Lucas, American Graffiti), and most versions say:
Somebody (Murch) asked for Reel 2, Dialog Track 2, in the abbreviated form "R-2-D2". Lucas, who was in the room and had dozed off while working on the script for *Star Wars*, momentarily woke when he heard the request and, after asking for clarification, stated that it was a "great name" before going back to writing his script. One more mystery of "The Force"?

# 3. Some Norms

The control of the source text can be done by checking if the text fulfills the corresponding/required norms. In this context it is vital to keep in mind that there is no universal norm for all countries/zones. There is a US-Norm, EU-Norm, Japanese-Norm, etc. In the following subchapters, three European norms will be indicated to show the complexity of this matter:
The European IEC/IEEE 82079-1:2019 Norm and
The European Hazardous Substances Ordinance and
The European New Product Liability Directive replacing the previous Product Liability Directive 85/374/EEC from 1985.

The idea some translation agencies have that a linguist can manage all norms because he is specialized in "technical industry" is far away from reality.

Identifying areas of interest or industries, such as legal, medical, technical, or literary translation are just a first step. Specialization goes deeper.

The same happens with "patent translations": patent translation is not only legal translation, but medical (with a lot of subchapters), industrial (with a lot of subchapters), biological (with a lot of subchapters) and so on, depending on the technical field of the invention. The linguist must know not only the legal requisites of a patent application, but also the field of the invention. Most times the field of the invention involves several subjects (medicine, orthopedics, fine mechanic, lubrication, etc.), so it is naive to say a linguist is expert in "patent translations" meaning only the legal aspect of the subject. This is never enough.

That's why specializing in a specific field enhances the expertise and marketability of the linguist expert.

# 3.1 IEC/IEEE 82079-1:2019 Preparation of Information for Use of Products

The standard [= norm DIN EN 82079-1] is a guide for instructions for use of products. In edition 2, with 130 pages, published on 2019-05, the international standard was presented by the technical committee ISO/T10/SC 1 to be revised. Below a copy of the Abstract:

| 3.1 | IEC/IEEE 82079-1:2019 Preparation of Information for Use (Instructions for Use) of Products |
|---|---|

<table>
<tr><td>Abstract</td></tr>
<tr><td>

IEC/IEEE 82079-1:2019 is jointly developed and published by IEC, IEEE, and ISO and provides general principles and detailed requirements for the design and formulation of all types of instructions for use that will be necessary or helpful for users of products of all kinds, ranging from a tin of paint to large or highly complex products, such as large industrial machinery, turnkey based plants or buildings. IEC/IEEE 82079-1:2019 cancels and replaces the first edition IEC 82079-1:2012. This edition constitutes a technical revision. It includes the following significant technical changes with respect to the previous edition:

a) The structure of this document has been rearranged in order to facilitate application of the standard and to make it easier to find information. Where possible, the language has been simplified.

b) Information for use is introduced as a generic term. Instructions for use is a synonym for information for use. Step-by-step instructions is used as a subset of information for use.

c) Clause 5 (principles) is revised and focuses on the purpose of information for use, the quality of information and the process for management of information.

d) The process for preparation of information for use is integrated in the normative part and addressed comprehensively.

e) Empirical methods for the evaluation of information for use are described in the normative part.

f) The professional competencies needed for the preparation of information for use are addressed more comprehensively.

g) Some aspects have been added to general requirements for information for use for complex systems of systems.

h) Consideration is given to instructions for self-assembly products.

i) An informative annex providing guidance on the fulfilment of specified requirements is introduced. This horizontal standard is primarily intended for use by technical committees in the preparation of standards in accordance with the principles laid down in IEC Guide 108. One of the responsibilities of a technical committee is, wherever applicable, to make use of horizontal standards in the preparation of its publications. The contents of this horizontal standard will not apply unless specifically referred to or included in the relevant publications.

</td></tr>
</table>

Source: Web

The translator doesn't have to know the whole norm and details, because it is "none of his business" as a translator. Other specialists are called to do the job (and assume the responsibility). However, it is possible that some translators are fluent in this matter, can work in this field and therefore are entitled to charge as a technical writer for this extra service. It is out of the question to expect the linguist to do the job without extra remuneration.

# 3.2 Hazardous Substances Ordinance

The ordinance regulates the protective measures for employees working with hazardous substances. The date of the original text is January 1, 1974. The date of the last amendment is January 1, 2005. The FAOLEX No. Is LEX-FAOC188739. It is amended by the Atomic Energy and Radiation Protection Act 5 of 2005 (Record updated on 2019-08-29). FAO means here Food and Agriculture Organization of the United Nations.

Hazardous substances are materials, mixtures, and products with certain (physical or chemical) dangerous properties.

In Germany, the ordinance came into effect on December 1, 2010.

For details see Directive 2014/27/EU and following revisions, amendments, and expansions (like the Biological Agents Ordinance and other occupational health and safety ordinances).

The ordinance is important for text writing and translations because the text has to be used as it is, no matter if correct or incorrect. Don't blame me!

| 3.2 | Trilingual example of a correct text |
|---|---|
| German | Gas/Rauch/Dampf/Aerosol nicht einatmen *(geeignete Bezeichnung(en) von Hersteller anzugeben)* |
| English | Do not breathe gas/fumes/vapour/spray *(appropriate wording to be specified by the manufacturer)* |
| Spanish | No respirar los gases/humos/vapores/aerosoles *(denominación(es) adecuada(s) a especificar por el fabricante)* |

Source: Hazardous Substances Ordinance, S23, as of reference date 2010

The wording corresponds in all three languages because it was correctly understood. The slashes mean there are options (1-4) to be specified or omitted by the manufacturer when necessary.

| 3.2 | Trilingual example of an incorrect text |
|---|---|
| German | Freisetzung in die Umwelt vermeiden. Besondere Anweisungen einholen/Sicherheitsdatenblatt zu Rate ziehen. |
| English | Avoid release to the environment. Refer to special instructions/Safety data sheet. |
| Spanish | Evítese su liberación al medio ambiente. Recábense instrucciones específicas de la ficha de datos de seguridad. |

Source: Hazardous Substances Ordinance, S61, as of reference date 2010

The wording doesn't correspond in all three languages because it was not correctly understood and <Safety> should read <safety>. The slash means there is the alternative to <refer to special instructions> or to <refer to safety data sheet>. This message is lost in Spanish.

## 3.3 The European New Product Liability Directive replacing the previous Product Liability Directive 85/374/EEC from 1985

On 28 September 2022, the European Commission published its proposal for a directive on liability of defective products revising the existing Product Liability Directive (PLD) that was adopted in 1985, nearly 40 years ago. The proposal aimed to bring the European Union's product liability regime up to speed with the digital age, and it also expresses the need to ease the burden of proof for consumers. Especially when consumers are seeking compensation for damages suffered because of defective products.

The Product Liability Directive (PLD) introduces the new concept of no-fault-based liability of producers for damage caused by defective products.

No-fault-based liability means that the liability does not depend on fault or negligence of the manufacturer.

To be compensated under the Product Liability Directive (PLD) no-fault liability regime, the burden of proof for the injured person is (strongly) simplified for the consumer.

State of the art: On October 10, 2024 the Council of the European Union adopted the new Directive on Liability for Defective Products.

Until the norm is implemented in national norms, there is no use to publish "the draft". Interested persons can however look on the web for the proposal in question under <The European New Product Liability Directive>.

# 4. Weighting

It was a scholar who used the term <vellones no tejidos> for the term <Vliesstoffe> stated in point 2.2. Example 8. The explanation he gave for his choice was a reference to Jason and The Argonauts and the epic journey to retrieve the golden fleece. Nice explanation, but not the technical term.

Scholars are not per se entitled to proofread a technical text. No matters if the text exists in a mono- or polylingual version. This is not only due to the complex nature of the text, of the technical field, and of other metalinguistic factors influencing the text functionality. A text can be good or bad for a single or multiple purpose(s). The text evaluation can be done by means of formal criteria (like counting linguistic mistakes, point subtraction for mistakes or point addition for best solutions, etc.) or by analysing the content of the text to see whether the message is clearly conveyed.

The "Birth Certificate" of a technical source text can be as shown below.

| 4. | The "Birth Certificate" of a technical source text |
|---|---|
| Step 1 | Invention, new model release, etc. needs documentation |
| Step 2 | Responsible department prepares the ""writing" |
| Step 3 | Responsible department contacts all other departments involved |
| Step 4 | First draft is created and sent to Technical Communication (or equivalent) |
| Step 5 | Technical Communication processes the draft 1 and creates draft 2 |
| Step 6 | Draft 2 goes back to the responsible department |
| | |
| Step 7 | All departments involved discuss draft 2 and release the master document file |
| Step 8 | Master document file is sent to the Linguistic Department (or equivalent) for translation |
| Step 9 | The master document file is distributed among the translators for translation |
| Own source. | |

In this case, we assume there is no formal error like misspelling, false interpunction, etc., and only functionality applies (because the source text was already spellchecked and proofread by different departments).

Skipping one or more steps, manufacturers shouldn't complain about suboptimal quality of the source text. The danger of "prenatal damage, mental illness, birth injury, miscarriage and stillbirth" in such cases is high.

As stated in point 2.2. Example 1, the translation of the source text can be a good one, but "unfunctional" and therefore useless for the purpose of the writing. In the abstract theory, there is no comprehensive framework for translation/text weighting. The theoretical approach from philosophical, linguistic, historical, and cultural perspectives (Jason and The Argonauts) doesn't apply, because there is no single objective way to measure text quality in this context. Either you know the technical term or not. If you know the technical term (or the company's term), you use it. If you don't know the technical term, you probably use the wrong term in almost every case if you are not a good linguistic expert knowing how to search for the right technical term (consulting the right source). The way is always case-related.

In our case we only consider the fulfillment of the text purpose. That means, only linguistic (right term) and metalinguistic (correct location of text and illustration, concordance between text and illustration, display, etc.) and multilingual functionability is relevant.

Multilingual functionability means not only translation, but also adaption. The source text can be static and dynamic. This fact must be considered in the translation.

If the text in the display of Example 1 is invariable (static), the concerned subjects (translators among others) should be a priori informed.

Point 2.2, Example 4 remains one of the most problematic areas of translation matters as a field of study, because it was/is never analyzed within this framework. Scholars and theorists take for granted that the source text is impeccable. Quality of source text was/is in most cases never measured.

The way how to proceed in such cases was/is never explained. There is no demand among scholars in this regard, even if it is one of the most interesting and controversial research areas in the field of translation. Indeed, it also belongs to the field of translation and scholars should take the whole context and conditions of translation into account.

The whole translation process (also what is before the proper process) should be explained and discussed during education and research. This analysis could help translators (linguistic experts) to adopt certain conscious strategies in real life which may bring them forwards in the profession.

Nobody tells students or linguistic experts how to act and react in such cases. Scholars and theorists provide no arguments for potential solutions. They don't even say (know) what market rates are. That means, how much linguistic experts should charge for such services, etc.

| See | Luis R. Cerna: CVs and Freelancers. Norderstedt 2024. ISBN 976-3-7597-4896-6. Point 4.1 Hourly rate. |
| --- | --- |

Direct freelancers' clients accept rates of 120 EUR/h (plus VAT). Agencies (intermediaries, exploiters) charge similar rates, but pay to the linguistic experts only 10-25 EUR/h (plus VAT).

| See | Luis R. Cerna: CVs and Freelancers. Norderstedt 2024. ISBN 976-3-7597-4896-6. Annex 2 "Profit Margins" Agencies and their profits. |
| --- | --- |

The above-mentioned Annex provides arguments for the interested linguistic expert and clearly illustrates the absurd situation for some linguistic expert working for agencies.

In general, the text purpose (function) can be to inform or to entertain. The industry or product specific information can aim at guiding subject X during a specific process, or informing about a new product, or a product list (catalog).

The industry specific source text can be good or bad for translation into one or more languages.

If the text is good for translation there will be no major problems of understanding and the translation can be ordered and executed.

If the source text is bad for translations, it will have to be revised and adapted before the translating step takes place.

Other factors like adaption to standards imperative for country/zone X must be done in one way or another before release.

As a general rule, scholars and theorists cannot easily evaluate the quality of a (technical) source text as herein stated because they don't necessarily have the objective parameters (i.e. technical knowledge) to carry out the effective source text quality weighting processes.

.

# 5. AI

During my education at the University of Heidelberg, students had to complete courses in traductology (translation science, St Hieronymus, father of translation, Vulgate, 382 AD) including text(ual) analysis and paraphrase. This allowed us to "play" with our corresponding three working languages consolidating in deep our linguistic knowledge. The output was, depending on the task, a content related text, a form related text, and/or an effect related text. Something AI cannot.

Here a definition of text analysis and paraphrase:

| 5. | Definition of text analysis and paraphrase |
|---|---|
| Text Analysis | The analysis in translation science means to determine whether the text is content related, meaning the purpose of the text is simply to convey information to the reader. Form related, meaning that the form, rhythm, and elegant phrasing of the text is essential, for example literature and poetry. Effect related, meaning the purpose of the text is to influence the reader in a certain direction, for example publicity. Of course, there are many mixed forms. |
| Paraphrase | The paraphrase or paraphrasing means to express the exact content of the text in different words. This is a very safe way to find out whether you completely understand/comprehend the text. |

Own source.

At that time we loved to create/use "twisters" like <no es lo mismo "el consulado general de Chile" que "el general con su chile de lado"> or <no es lo mismo "una paloma en el Canal de la Mancha" que "una mancha en el canal de la paloma"> or <no es lo mismo "verla venir" que "platicar con ella">.

Concerning <Canal de la Mancha>, the reader must allow me to stress that this is a classical unerasable and wrong translation of French <(Canal de) La Manche> and the English name <English Channel> is a casus belli for the French people. For details, see: Antoine Augustin B de La Martiniere: Le grand Dictionnnaire géographique et critique. 1768.

We also talked of <Juan Sebastián Arroyo> and his music. Think of "Evil Under the Sun" by Agatha Christie (1941, Giuseppe Verdi and the allusion to the last name "Green" in the book) or the well know question "to whom did Beathoven (sc.) dedicate his fifth symphony?", answer "to his father!", think of the beginning of the symphony "para papa, para papa" (this works only in Spanish).

Hereinafter we take AI into consideration when used for writing a text, translating a text, and interpreting a speech.

## 5.1 Writing a Text

Writing a text means generating in your mind a text before writing it down in one language for a specific purpose, while AI writing means putting together text blocks in one language according to certain rules set by someone.

The output is a text in a specific language with a specific purpose. The author tries to build a text with logic and intelligence.

In this context, AI can be used as a tool or as an author.

The use as a tool can be good for research, putting facts together, etc., before the author generates a text in one language or more for a specific purpose.

The use of AI as an author can be tricky if the claiming author doesn't specify the algorithm source and percentage of "his" work.

The criterium for the work is "good enough for the purpose!"

There is nothing you get more easily and faster used to as mediocrity! In other words, mediocrity becomes the new standard!

Copyright standards should be observed.

Now here an interesting perspective about AI writing and publishing:
It is a long-time fact that the way the large AI companies have accepted and stolen the intellectual property of millions of authors is dreadful and illegal, but who has the money and perseverance to fight them?

Some well-known authors have done so, but that hasn't stopped the AI companies continuing their mass theft.

Some suggestions:
Take back your agency and decide whether you want to participate in the theft
If you decide to participate, make a conscious decision, and weigh up the value exchange you get in return,
You still can decide not to play this game
You can protect your IP.
You can publish and promote your book in different ways.
Evaluate what you publish and share and what you put behind a paywall on the web.
Avoid to make contents easily available.
Don't sign any contract before consulting your lawyer.
Make yourself aware of what your options are.
These are no easy or simple decisions, but they are yours to make, and you need to make yourself aware of what your options are and choose.

| See | 5.6 Documentation of the Time Factor! |
| --- | --- |

## 5.2 Translating a Text

Translating a text from language A into language B means transferring in written form the content, form, and effect of text A into text B, while AI translating means putting together in written form text blocks according to certain language concordances set by someone (not necessarily a linguist).

The output of a translator is a more or less concordant text. Within the quality assurance, the output can be improved or aggravated, depending on the qualification of the proofreader.

The output of an AI translation is mostly a discordance text in another language that needs to be reedited. The criterium for the translation is usually "good enough for the purpose!"

There is nothing you get more easily and faster used to as mediocrity! In other words, mediocrity becomes the new standard!

All considerations stated in in point <5.1 Writing a Text> concerning the mass theft of intellectual property also apply to translating a text via AI.

Copyright standards should be observed.

| See | 5.6 Documentation of the Time Factor! |
|-----|----------------------------------------|

## 5.3 Interpreting a Speech

Interpreting a speech from language A into language B means oral transmission of the content, form, and effect of the speech from language A into language B, while AI interpreting means putting together speech blocks according to certain language concordances set by someone.

The output is a concordance/discordance speech in another language.

In the United States, broadcast stations frequently use computer interpretation of political speeches or statements in the news or political programs to show to the audience what aliens think of a specific problem (sometimes with the same computer-generated voice). The criterium for the interpretation is "good enough for the purpose!"

On April 2025 I heard a radio program show where a statement of Emmanuel Macron (the French president at that time) was AI-interpreted. I almost had a heart attack listening to Macron speaking English with a computer-generated voice and his typical French inflection and speed. Macron speaking English with his French speed (like a submachine gun) and inflection, that was offending, but there is nothing you get more easily and faster used to as mediocrity! In other words, mediocrity becomes the new standard!

What do I mean by this? Let me explain it to you this way: the working languages of my wlfe are German, English and Spanish (it doesn't mean she speaks only the three languages) with the corresponding native accent. She speaks Hochdeutsch, UK- and US-English, and international Spanish, and for each language version she has a "different voice, melody, inflection, speed, etc."

Copyright standards should be observed.

| See | 5.6 Documentation of the Time Factor! |
|-----|---------------------------------------|

## 5.4 Concordances to AI

By the way, I am against the concordance <AI = Artificial Intelligence> because it is simply thoughtless.

Artificial intelligence is not an undisputed term in linguistics. The main problem resides in how the term is used in other less critical technical fields or what the users reflect in the term.

The semantic is different depending on the purpose of the users and on the theoretical framework.

| 5.4 | Definition of intelligence |
|---|---|
| Cambridge Dictionary | The ability to learn, understand, and make judgments or have opinions that are based on reason. |
| Oxford Languages | The ability to acquire and apply knowledge and skills. |
| Collins Dictionary | The ability to think, reason, and understand instead of doing things automatically or by instinct. |

Own source.

My favorite definition is the one given by the Collins Dictionary, but this is my subjective point of view:

| 5.4 | Definition of algorithm |
|---|---|
| Web 1 | A process or set of rules to be followed in calculations or other problem-solving operations. |
| Web 2 | A sequence of instructions that a computer must perform to solve a well-defined problem. |
| Web 3 | A step-by-step process that is completed the same way every time. |
| Web 4 | A limited number of steps that effectively generate a result (bunny rabbit knot; following a recipe; finding a library book in the library). |

Own source.

In other words, it is a routine to be processed the same way every time to obtain a specific result.

| 5.4 | Definition of input |
|---|---|
| Oxford Languages | What is put in, taken in, or operated on by any process or system. |

Own source.

In our case, what is operated on by an algorithm.

AI means <algorithm input> and has nothing to do with human intelligence. It is a technology that allows computers to perform defined tasks that typically require the treatment of a lot of data in short time.

# 5.5 Documentation of the Time Factor

The market is saturated with AI tools for publishing, translating, and interpreting. Most people (not experts in the mentioned fields of publishing, translation, and interpreting, of course) think the work is afterwards all done because such tools are supposed to be fast, reliable, accessible, and seemingly easy to use, and are surprised when the invoice for revision arrives. But they end up costing the job poster more time (and money) than expected. Remember my wording about mediocrity!

To avoid unnecessarily disputes with the job poster, it is fundamental to document the time the revisor needed for each phase of the job.

Below you find a Table for documentation of the time factor for the different phases of the revision. Due to the nature of some texts, i.e. specific working phases are not for the public, I leave some lines empty the owner of a copy of my book can use for and adapt to his requirements if he/she is so nice to keep my copyright at the bottom of the Table.

| Number | Task | Time in min. |
|:---:|:---|:---:|
| 01 | Reformatting | |
| 02 | Redoing the layout | |
| 03 | Fixing errors in logic | |
| 04 | Fixing errors in grammar | |
| 05 | Fixing errors in technical messages/instructions | |
| 06 | Taking advantage of previously validated content | |
| 07 | Saving the quality | |
| 08 | Keeping alive the brand voice | |
| 09 | Gaining control over the process | |
| 10 | Checking for hallucinations | |
| 11 | Recapturing the brand's tone | |
| 12 | | |
| 13 | | |
| 14 | | |
| 15 | | |
| 16 | | |
| 17 | | |
| 18 | | |
| 19 | | |
| 20 | | |
| 21 | | |
| 22 | | |
| 23 | | |
| 24 | | |
| 25 | | |

© Luis R. Cerna 2025